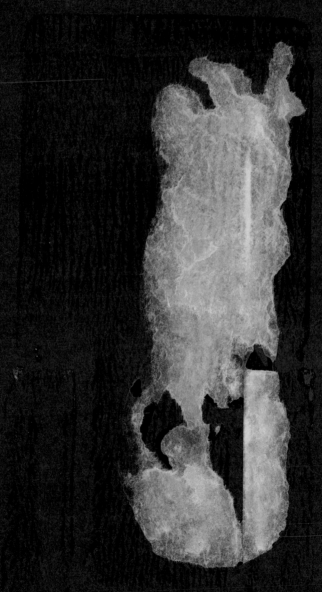

M

THREE SECRET POEMS

ΤΡΙΑ ΚΡΥΦΑ ΠΟΙΗΜΑΤΑ

THREE SECRET POEMS

BY GEORGE SEFERIS

Translated from the Greek
by Walter Kaiser

Harvard University Press
Cambridge, Massachusetts

1969

CONTENTS

Translator's Foreword   vii

THREE SECRET POEMS

    On a Ray of Winter Sun   3

    On Stage   19

    Summer Solstice   35

Notes   67

Acknowledgments   71

TRANSLATOR'S FOREWORD

The poems translated in this book are the most recent work of Greece's greatest living poet. Published in Athens in December, 1966, they are the first new poems by George Seferis to have appeared in something over a decade. That decade, in retrospect, exhibits a number of important milestones in Seferis' long career as author and diplomat. During that period he served for five years as his country's ambassador to Great Britain and then, in 1962, retired from the diplomatic service. The year of his retirement also saw the publication of his monograph on Delphi and his revised collection of essays written over the preceding quarter-century. In the following year, Seferis was awarded the Nobel Prize for Literature. Subsequently, he published several short prose works, including his *Discours de Stockholm*, and two volumes of translations from T. S. Eliot; at the same time, he was at work on his translations of The Song of Songs and The Apocalypse of St. John, both of which were to appear in the same year as *Three Secret Poems*. Finally, toward the end of this decade he prepared for publication a collection of his translations from French and English poetry and, most important, the monumental collected edition of his own poetry from 1922 to 1955.

In certain respects, then, these poems witness a critical moment in Seferis' career. The first poetry since his retirement from public life, they come just after he had surveyed and re-edited all his previous writing. The question that must inevitably confront a poet at such a time of reassessment is that of where and how to go forward, and indeed several sections of *Three Secret Poems* attest to this preoccupation. Hence it is not surprising that these poems, though they form an integral part of Seferis' total *oeuvre*, manifest as well a number of new departures, both in style and in mood. Unhappily, one cannot properly discuss, with reference to a translation, the ways in which language is here employed in a new, highly personal, almost "secret" fashion; nor can one adequately describe such elements as the rhythmic innovations that distinguish these poems from their predecessors. Even in translation, however, it is possible to perceive the shorter lines, the extraordinary economy of means, the compressed lyric intensity, and the greater general austerity of this latest work. Poetry here has been stripped to its naked essence, as if in response to a wish expressed in an earlier poem:

> All I want is to speak simply; may I be given this grace.
> For even the song we have burdened with so much
>   music that bit by bit it sinks,
> and our craft, we have embellished it so much that its
>   face is eaten away by the gold;
> and it is time for us to say our very few words, for
>   tomorrow our soul sets sail.
>
> ("An Old Man on the River Bank")

It is just this quality of utmost simplicity and candor — a quality sought also by the late Yeats — which gives these *Three Secret Poems* their special luminosity and places them among Seferis' most profoundly moving, most intensely personal utterances.

Like everything else Seferis has written, these poems are deeply rooted in the Greek world, nourished, as he says, with its earth and rock, informed with its myths and culture, haunted by its past glories and present misery. Yet it is also characteristic that their relevance immediately extends far beyond any boundaries, whether national, cultural, or temporal, to make them meaningful for all men, a possession (in the words of an earlier Greek) for all time. This is what makes the poetry of Seferis truly classical, in the best sense of that much abused term: the universal is contained within and exfoliates out from the particular, and neither exists independent of the other. Thus, in his poetic vision, the journey of one soul becomes the journey of all souls; the anguish of one war, that of all wars; the love of one woman, that of all mankind. The sea, which ebbs and flows through his poetry from the beginning, is in reality all seas, geographical or metaphorical; at the same time, it is always specifically the Aegean, that uniquely blue, uniquely storied, uniquely tragic sea. Even the sun, which plays such a dominant role in these poems, though it is the universal source of light, is always specifically the Grecian sun with its peculiar intensity and clarity, its particular terrors.

This aspect of Seferis' poetry presents a special kind of difficulty for both the translator and the non-Greek reader. Whereas normally in poetry of such classicism we perceive the particular and move on from there to the universal, in this case the process is curiously reversed. Most probably, it is the general applicability of Seferis' message which reaches us first, as these poems become almost instantaneously *our* poems and we relate them to our own experience of the world. To see how they are also *his* poems, to comprehend, that is, how they grow out of the personal and specific experiences of an individual Greek — this is what poses the greater difficulty for a foreigner. What is universal in his poetry we test on our very pulse; what is personal and local we can, at best, only experience vicariously.

Of course, such cultural distances and diffractions always trouble translations. When, for example, Flaubert writes in a letter that one of his heroines is "tendre comme du pain frais," the simile proves untranslatable to the world of Wonder Bread and Pepperidge Farm. Its meaning depends on a culture where bread has an importance it does not here, where local bakers offer you a half-dozen different sizes, shapes, textures, and flavors, where housewives go out to buy their bread for each separate meal. But the world of Greece is even more remote than that of France for the Anglo-Saxon reader. That vast integument of history, custom, folklore, natural phenomena, and topography which tacitly envelops the poetry of Seferis is something that we, unlike his countrymen, can know only at second hand. Language invariably reflects such distances, and like all languages Modern Greek has its words — δροσιά, καημός, γλυκοχάραμα, παλικάρι — for which there are no equivalents in any other tongue. Yet it is the world-wide, everyday words that set the real snares for reader and translator — words like *bread* and *wine, sun* and *sea,* which call up different images and emotions to the non-Greek and the Greek.

To say the same thing in a less complicated way is simply to acknowledge that certain basic resonances of Seferis' poetry are accessible only to the Greek or, perhaps, to the reader who has known the world of Greece personally. For example, even so easy a phrase as "the stars . . . which trod upon your nakedness one night," though it is adequately comprehensible, achieves its full impact only for someone who has experienced the palpable closeness of stars in those latitudes. So, too, the way in which "the sea wind and the coolness of dawn" can perform a benediction in that hot land, the present immediacy of such deities of the past as Hecate, the Graiae, and the Furies, the complex of folkloristic associations that center on a feast day like that of St. John — all such things are intuitively understood by the reader for whom they are part of daily life.

I do not mean to overemphasize such difficulties, but it is important to recognize that they are there, especially because they are inherent in the predominant image in *Three Secret Poems,* that of the sun. In his later poetry, the sun has become one of Seferis' most complex symbols, and for the northerner to understand its full implications requires a considerable effort of the imagination. It is not merely that our sun is more pallid than his or that we in the north seek the sun in summer while Greeks seek the shade. Perhaps one can come closer to its meaning for Seferis if one recalls that the tragedies of English drama take place at midnight, whereas those of Greek drama reach their catastrophe at high noon:

the bloodstained worlds of Macbeth and Orestes exist at the antipodes of night and day. W. H. Auden, in one of his finest poems, says farewell to the island of Ischia; observing that "the Greeks used to call the Sun / He-who-smites-from-afar," he comments on the hopelessness of life under such an unchanging, inescapable source of heat and brightness. Auden, however, is writing about the Italian *mezzogiorno* and the despair of its relentless sun; the intenser sun of the Greek μεσημέρι brings, beyond despair, tragic terror. I myself remember a moment under the blazing sun on a bare Cycladic hill when I first understood what the Panic hour really is — a moment infinitely more terrifying and minatory than childhood's dark nights.

For Seferis, the Greek sun is this ultimate paradox, both life-giver and death-bringer, desired and feared, "angelic" and "black." "You stare into the sun, then you are lost in the darkness," he says in one of his poems, and, in a vivid image recurrent in his poetry, he compares the experience to that of the animal who stares blindly into the approaching headlights that bring his death. According to Heraclitus (the "ripple" of whose great soul, Seferis says elsewhere, "is still perceptible in our thought"), Hades and Dionysus are the same; at the heart of light there is darkness. Seferis' fullest statement of this paradox is beautifully set forth in the last section of his great poem, "The Thrush," and in a letter to George Katsimbalis commenting on this poem, he explains:

> I have a very organic feeling that identifies humaneness with the Greek landscape . . . it is my belief that in the Greek light there is a kind of process of

humanization; I think of Aeschylus not as the Titan or the Cyclops that people sometimes want us to see him as, but as a man feeling and expressing himself close beside us, accepting or reacting to the natural elements just as we all do. I think of the mechanism of justice which he sets before us, this alternation of Hubris and Ate, which one will not find to be simply a moral law unless it is also a law of nature . . . Heraclitus will declare: "The sun will not overstep his measures; if he does, the Erinyes, the handmaids of Justice, will find him out."

The Erinyes will hunt down the sun just as they hunted down Orestes; just think of these cords which unite man with the elements of nature, this tragedy that is in nature and in man at the same time, this intimacy. Suppose the light were suddenly to become Orestes? It is so easy, just think: if the light of the day and the blood of man were one and the same thing? How far can one stretch this feeling? "Just anthropomorphism," people say, and they pass on. I do not think it is as simple as that.*

It is the wintry absence of this sun that occasions, and mirrors, the haunting mood of despair in which these *Three Secret Poems* begin. More than mere seasonal description, the stark, cold, etiolated landscape of the first poem serves to reflect a personal state of soul and the general desolation of the modern world. In this win-

* "Letter on 'The *Thrush*'," in *On the Greek Style. Selected Essays in Poetry and Hellenism*, trans. Rex Warner and Th. D. Frangopoulos (Boston and Toronto, 1966), pp. 103–105.

ter of discontent, the paralyzed spirit finds that the past is lifeless, its voices become petrified playthings for children, its dancers arrested, its sea nymphs metamorphosed into bleached seaweed, its books and papers useless. The present is a time of rusted tin and angry gulls, of maddening companions and numbing darkness, intolerable to the poet who longs for his true element, the light. Only near the end of the poem, as the poet finally rejects the books and papers of the past and strains for a new vision of life (characteristically expressed by Seferis in mythological terms) does he feel the first vernal winds of rebirth and perceive a ray of sun. Somewhat analogous to the experience described by Eliot at the beginning of "Little Gidding," this brief instant of life-giving sun becomes a still, timeless moment in which hope for the future redeems the agony of past and present and the sunbeam itself is transformed into a Heraclitan flash of lightning.

Yet the longed-for sun, when it does come at the beginning of the second poem, turns out to be not the simple, vivifying dance that had been anticipated, but something more complex and ominous. The nakedness of so much light is the darkness of blood, the obscurity of such dense, bewildering forests as those in which Erophile and Dante were lost. The poet imagines himself seated in the empty ruins of an ancient amphitheater, like those, now fallen prey to poppies and lizards, which are scattered along the Ionian coasts of Seferis' boyhood. A passage from a diary kept in 1950, when he returned to his former home in Asia Minor, serves as a gloss on this poem:

Theatre of Hierapolis, theatre of Stratonikeia, theatre of Pergamum, theatre of Ephesus. You tried to imagine the rows of eyes in the audiences of these theatres, how they would appear. You think of them now as evening falls, and they seem to you like shells in the hands of children. In this theatre there has been played for you a tragedy without a catastrophe, because it was never allowed to find its purification. The sun sinks below the rocks of The Two Brothers. The twilight spreads over the sky and the sea the colours of an inexhaustible love. And you are ashamed because you want to howl aloud that it is all a gigantic lie. Because you know that the circle has never closed, and that the Furies, who in this small and remote place were let loose upon the strong and the weak of the earth, have not been laid to rest, and you will not see them, nor will your children, "vanish into the depths of the earth." *

In a strophe from his previous collection of poems, Seferis once again imagines an experience in such a theater:

> Even now I remember:
> he was journeying to Ionian coasts, to empty shells of
>   theaters,
> where only the lizard glides over dry stones,
> and I asked him: "Will they ever be full again?"
> And he answered me: "Perhaps, at the hour of death."
> And he ran across the orchestra howling:

* "The Other World," trans. Ian Scott-Kilvert, *The London Magazine*, VI (August, 1966), 62–63. The quotation at the end of this passage is from Aeschylus' *Eumenides*.

"Let me hear my brother!"
And it was harsh, the silence around us,
blank on the glass of the blue.

("Memory II")

Here, in the second of *Three Secret Poems*, as he sits
in the amphitheater, those nameless, foreboding mes-
sengers who have come into Seferis' poetry again and
again from the earliest poems unexpectedly arrive, as the
theater suddenly fills and the stage lights dim. In the
terrifying, hallucinatory drama that now unfolds, the poet
engages in an unspoken dialogue with the protago-
nist, who identifies herself with the sea. But the sea
itself, once a source of boyhood happiness and poetic
inspiration, has become desolate and infected, despite
the hope that had once been extended by the Protean
Old Man of the Sea (another recurrent figure in Seferis'
poetry). That hope, the next section suggests, has been
destroyed in what Seferis elsewhere describes as "un-
lucky times: wars, destructions, exiles." The reference
is not only to the infamous tragedy at Smyrna in 1922
but also to the greater slaughter it heralded, the Second
World War, of which Seferis has written more movingly
than any other poet. Following this, the poem introduces
one of the book's dominant themes, a theme hinted at
once or twice before but only now fully articulated: the
problem of the poet in what another lover of Greece,
Hölderlin, once described as "dürftiger Zeit." Employing
a meditative cadence we have not heard before in these
poems, Seferis speaks poignantly of the process of poetic
creation and, with an unforgettable simile of wind-
shaped pines, of the ultimate value of poetry for man.

A challenging question leads to the apocalyptic, sun-flooded vision of the final section of this poem, perhaps the most beautiful single lyric in *Three Secret Poems*.

The last of the three poems brings us to the eve of the summer solstice, the brief darkness before the day of brightest sun and longest light. An initial, Dantesque vision of the world as threshing-floor — an image dear to Seferis — gives way to a sequence of nightmares depicting the debased, meretricious modern world of the present in all its tawdry cheapness and paralyzing aridity. As he stands in his Athenian garden, the poet's nocturnal meditations raise once again the spectral question of how to write in such a ruined time, and he finds that the answer lies in a resigned acceptance of self and his own stony ground which, like Odysseus' Ithaca, is harsh but nourishing. In the magnificent, plangent verses that follow, the poet, confronting what Mallarmé called "le vide papier que la blancheur défend," finds that the blank page, while it cruelly mirrors all that is past, also offers the one hope of redeeming that past. Dawn breaks, fragile and vulnerable, but bringing a dream of hope "at the hour when dreams come true." Over the summer sea and the islands of the Saronic Gulf, the heat gathers with thrilling intensity as the sun rises to its zenith, and in the blinding light of midday, at the very moment when life seems to stop altogether, the pangs of rebirth are felt.

The concluding section of the poem brings us to the full noon of the summer solstice, the year's turning point, celebrated by Greeks as the Feast of St. John Lambrophoros, "bringer of light." Through their progress from the depths of winter to the height of summer, these poems have moved out of the darkness into the light; the faint "occasional glimmerings" of the first poem have grown into the refulgent flames of the sun and bonfires in the last, where "everything wants to burn." In this final conflagration, it is right that all should be consumed and destroyed; for all is, at the same time, purified and reborn, as the ashes are sown anew. Triumphing over the agonizing nightmares of the present and the erosion of time's muddy river, these timeless flames of purification rise in transcendent hope. The miracle of these poems, like that of Sophocles' and Shakespeare's last plays, is that they encompass so much suffering and despair and yet can appropriately end on this note of ultimate affirmation.

Along with everything else he has written, these *Three Secret Poems* form part of Seferis' life-long quest for self-discovery. As the celebrated injunction that once stood over the portals at Delphi suggests, that quest is a peculiarly Greek endeavor. This too, in some mysterious, ineffable way, is the challenge of the Greek landscape, which every traveler there has felt: its demand that you come to terms not only with its past but also with your own. To know and accept who one really is, to understand one's place in history, to create poetry out of tragic times, to learn the meaning of love, to persist in the long journey — these are the perpetual concerns of Seferis' work. And his great themes are the eternal themes of poetry: love and war, voyage and exile, death and rebirth, sea and sun. "I am," he once wrote, "a monotonous and obstinate sort of man who . . . has gone on saying the same things over and over again." They are, of course, simply the same things that history itself has unceasingly reiterated, but Seferis' profound achievement has been to understand that message and give it expression in our epoch. In *Three Secret Poems* he states it once more, with renewed vigor and penetrating vision. There has never been a time when we needed more desperately to ponder it.

THREE SECRET POEMS

ΠΑΝΩ ΣΕ ΜΙΑ ΧΕΙΜΩΝΙΑΤΙΚΗ ΑΧΤΙΝΑ

ON A RAY OF WINTER SUN

Α΄

Φύλλα ἀπὸ σκουριασμένο τενεκὲ
γιὰ τὸ φτωχὸ μυαλὸ ποὺ εἶδε τὸ τέλος·
τὰ λιγοστὰ λαμπυρίσματα.
Φύλλα ποὺ στροβιλίζουνται μὲ γλάρους
ἀγριεμένους μὲ τὸ χειμώνα.

Ὅπως ἐλευθερώνεται ἕνα στῆθος
οἱ χορευτὲς ἔγιναν δέντρα
ἕνα μεγάλο δάσος γυμνωμένα δέντρα.

1.

Leaves of rusted tin
for the poor brain that has seen the end:
occasional glimmerings.
Leaves whirled with the gulls
angry at winter.

Just as a breast is freed
the dancers become trees,
a huge forest of bared trees.

B´

Καίγουνται τ' ἄσπρα φύκια
Γραῖες ἀναδυόμενες χωρὶς βλέφαρα
σχήματα ποὺ ἄλλοτε χορεύαν
μαρμαρωμένες φλόγες.
Τὸ χιόνι σκέπασε τὸν κόσμο.

2.

The white seaweed is burned:
Graiae rising up without eyelids,
shapes that in another time danced,
flames become marble.
Snow covered the world.

Γ΄

Οἱ σύντροφοι μ' εἴχαν τρελάνει
μὲ θεοδόλιχους ἐξάντες πετροκαλαμῆθρες
καὶ τηλεσκόπια ποὺ μεγαλώναν πράγματα —
καλύτερα νὰ μέναν μακριά.
Ποῦ θὰ μᾶς φέρουν τέτιοι δρόμοι;
Ὅμως ἡ μέρα ἐκείνη ποὺ ἄρχισε
μπορεῖ δὲν ἔσβησε ἀκόμη
μὲ μιὰ φωτιὰ σ' ἕνα φαράγγι σὰν τριαντάφυλλο
καὶ μιὰ θάλασσα ἀνάερη στὰ πόδια τοῦ Θεοῦ.

3.

The companions had driven me mad
with theodolites, sextants, lodestones,
and telescopes that enlarged things —
better such things should stay distant.
Where will they lead us, such roads?
But that day which began
is perhaps not yet extinguished,
with fire in a ravine like a rose
and a weightless sea at the feet of God.

Δ΄

Εἶπες ἐδῶ καὶ χρόνια:
«Κατὰ βάθος εἶμαι ζήτημα φωτός».
Καὶ τώρα ἀκόμη σὰν ἀκουμπᾶς
στὶς φαρδιὲς ὠμοπλάτες τοῦ ὕπνου
ἀκόμη κι' ὅταν σὲ ποντίζουν
στὸ ναρκωμένο στῆθος τοῦ πελάγου
ψάχνεις γωνιὲς ὅπου τὸ μαῦρο
ἔχει τριφτεῖ καὶ δὲν ἀντέχει
ἀναζητᾶς ψηλαφητὰ τὴ λόγχη
τὴν ὁρισμένη νὰ τρυπήσει τὴν καρδιά σου
γιὰ νὰ τὴν ἀνοίξει στὸ φῶς.

4.

Years ago you said,
"In essence, I am matter of light."
And even now, whenever you rest
on the broad shoulders of sleep,
or even when they cast you
on the numb breast of the sea,
you seek corners where the blackness
has worn off and does not persist;
groping, you search for the appointed spear
to pierce your heart
that it may open to the light.

Ε΄

Ποιὸς βουρκωμένος ποταμὸς μᾶς πῆρε;
Μείναμε στὸ βυθό.
Τρέχει τὸ ρέμα πάνω ἀπ᾽ τὸ κεφάλι μας
λυγίζει τ᾽ ἄναρθρα καλάμια·

οἱ φωνὲς
κάτω ἀπ᾽ τὴν καστανιὰ γίναν χαλίκια
καὶ τὰ πετᾶνε τὰ παιδιά.

5.

What muddy river bore us away?
We remained in the depths.
The current flows over our heads,
bending the mute reeds;

the voices
under the chestnut tree have become pebbles,
and the children throw them.

ς'

Μικρὴ πνοὴ κι' ἄλλη πνοή, σπιλιάδα
καθὼς ἀφήνεις τὸ βιβλίο
καὶ σκίζεις ἄχρηστα χαρτιὰ τῶν περασμένων
ἢ σκύβεις νὰ κοιτάξεις στὸ λιβάδι
ἀγέρωχους κενταύρους ποὺ καλπάζουν
ἢ ἄγουρες ἀμαζόνες ἱδρωμένες
σ' ὅλα τ' αὐλάκια τοῦ κορμιοῦ
ποὺ ἔχουν ἀγώνα τὸ ἄλμα καὶ τὴν πάλη.

Ἀναστάσιμες σπιλιάδες μιὰν αὐγὴ
ποὺ νόμισες πὼς βγῆκε ὁ ἥλιος.

6.

A small breath of air, and then another, gusts
as you abandon the book
and tear up the useless papers of the past
or try to distinguish in the pasture
arrogant centaurs galloping
or young amazons
engaged in jumping and wrestling,
sweat in every furrow of their bodies.

Gusts of resurrection one dawn
when you thought the sun came out.

Z'

Τὴ φλόγα τὴ γιατρεύει ἡ φλόγα
ὄχι μὲ τῶν στιγμῶν τὸ στάλαγμα
ἀλλὰ μιὰ λάμψη, μονομιᾶς·
ὅπως ὁ πόθος ποὺ ἔσμιξε τὸν ἄλλο πόθο
κι' ἀπόμειναν καθηλωμένοι
ἢ ὅπως
ρυθμὸς τῆς μουσικῆς ποὺ μένει
ἐκεῖ στὸ κέντρο σὰν ἄγαλμα

ἀμετάθετος.

Δὲν εἶναι πέρασμα τούτη ἡ ἀνάσα
οἰακισμὸς κεραυνοῦ.

7.

Flame is healed by flame,
not through the stillicide of seconds
but all at once, in a flash;
like the desire that mingled with the other desire
and remained transfixed,
or like
the rhythm of music that remains
there in the center like a statue,

motionless.

It is not a passage, this breathing,
but a tiller-thrust of lightning.

ΕΠΙ ΣΚΗΝΗΣ

ON STAGE

Α΄

Ἥλιε παίζεις μαζί μου
κι᾽ ὅμως δὲν εἶναι τοῦτο χορὸς
ἡ τόση γύμνια
αἷμα σχεδὸν
γι᾽ ἄγριο κανένα δάσο·
τότε —

1.

You are playing with me, sun;
and yet, this is not a dance:
so much nakedness
is almost blood,
or some wild forest;
and then —

Β΄

Σήμαντρα ἀκούστηκαν
κι' ἦρθαν οἱ μαντατοφόροι·
δὲν τοὺς περίμενα
λησμονημένη κι' ἡ λαλιά τους·
ξεκούραστοι φρεσκοντυμένοι
κρατώντας κάνιστρα τοὺς καρπούς.
Θαύμασα καὶ ψιθύρισα:
«Μ' ἀρέσουν τ' ἀμφιθέατρα».
Ἡ ἀχιβάδα γέμισε ἀμέσως
καὶ χαμήλωσε τὸ φῶς στὴ σκηνὴ
ὅπως γιὰ κάποιο περιώνυμο φονικό.

2.

Gongs sounded
and the messengers came.
I was not expecting them;
even their voices were forgotten.
They came rested, freshly clothed,
bearing baskets of fruit.
I marveled, murmuring,
"Amphitheaters delight me."
The shell filled at once
and the stage lights dimmed,
as if for some notorious slaughter.

Γ´

Ἐσὺ τί γύρευες; Τραυλὴ στὴν ὄψη.
Μόλις ποὺ εἶχες σηκωθεῖ
ἀφήνοντας τὰ σεντόνια νὰ παγώσουν
καὶ τὰ ἐκδικητικὰ λουτρά.
Στάλες κυλούσαν στοὺς ὤμους σου
στὴν κοιλιά σου
τὰ πόδια σου κατάσαρκα στὸ χῶμα
στὸ θερισμένο χόρτο.
Ἐκεῖνοι, τρεῖς
τὰ πρόσωπα τῆς τολμηρῆς Ἑκάτης.
Γύρευαν νὰ σὲ πάρουν μαζί τους.
Τὰ μάτια σου δυὸ τραγικὰ κοχύλια
κι᾽ εἶχες στὶς ρόγες στὰ βυζιὰ
δυὸ βυσσινιὰ μικρὰ χαλίκια —
σύνεργα τῆς σκηνῆς, δὲν ξέρω.
Ἐκεῖνοι ἀλάλαζαν
ἔμενες ριζωμένη στὸ χῶμα·
σκίζαν τὸν ἀέρα τὰ νοήματά τους.
Δοῦλοι τοὺς ἔφεραν τὰ μαχαίρια·
ἔμενες ριζωμένη στὸ χῶμα
κυπαρίσσι.
Ἔσυραν τὰ μαχαίρια ἀπ᾽ τὰ θηκάρια
κι᾽ ἔψαχναν ποῦ νὰ σὲ χτυπήσουν.
Τότε μονάχα φώναξες:
«Ἂς ἔρθει νὰ μὲ κοιμηθεῖ ὅποιος θέλει,
μήπως δὲν εἶμαι ἡ θάλασσα;»

3.

You, what were you seeking? Your face grimaced.
You had just arisen,
leaving the sheets to grow cold
and the avenging baths.
Drops rolled over your shoulders,
over your belly,
your feet bare on the ground,
on the cut grass.
They,
the three faces of bold Hecate,
they sought to take you with them.
Your eyes were two tragic shells,
and on the nipples of your breasts you had
two small cherry-red pebbles —
stage props, I suppose.
They,
they howled,
but you remained rooted to the ground;
their gestures tore the air.
Slaves brought them knives,
but you remained rooted to the ground,
a cypress.
They drew the knives from the scabbards
and probed where to strike you.
Only then did you cry out:
"Let whoever wishes come sleep with me:
am I not the sea?"

Δ´

Ἡ θάλασσα· πῶς ἔγινε ἔτσι ἡ θάλασσα;
Ἄργησα χρόνια στὰ βουνά·
μὲ τύφλωσαν οἱ πυγολαμπίδες.
Τώρα σὲ τοῦτο τ᾿ ἀκρογιάλι περιμένω
ν᾿ ἀράξει ἔνας ἄνθρωπος
ἔνα ὑπόλειμμα, μιὰ σχεδία.

Μὰ μπορεῖ νὰ κακοφορμίσει ἡ θάλασσα;
Ἕνα δελφίνι τὴν ἔσκισε μιὰ φορὰ
κι᾿ ἀκόμη μιὰ φορὰ
ἡ ἄκρη τοῦ φτεροῦ ἑνὸς γλάρου.

Κι᾿ ὅμως εἶταν γλυκὸ τὸ κύμα
ὅπου ἔπεφτα παιδὶ καὶ κολυμπούσα
κι᾿ ἀκόμη σὰν ἤμουν παλικάρι
καθὼς ἔψαχνα σχήματα στὰ βότσαλα,
γυρεύοντας ρυθμούς,
μοῦ μίλησε ὁ Θαλασσινὸς Γέρος:
«Ἐγώ εἶμαι ὁ τόπος σου·
ἴσως νὰ μὴν εἶμαι κανεὶς
ἀλλὰ μπορῶ νὰ γίνω αὐτὸ ποὺ θέλεις».

4.

The sea: how did it become so, the sea?
For years I lingered in the mountains;
the fireflies blinded me.
Now, on this shore, I wait
for the arrival of a man,
a raft, flotsam.

Can it be, though, that the sea has become infected?
A dolphin lanced it once,
and another time
the tip of a gull's wing.

Yet the wave was sweet
where I dived and swam as a child,
and when, a young man,
I looked for patterns in pebbles,
seeking rhythms,
the Old Man of the Sea said to me:
"I am your land;
perhaps I am no one,
yet I can become what you wish."

Ε'

Ποιὸς ἄκουσε καταμεσήμερα
τὸ σύρσιμο τοῦ μαχαιριοῦ στὴν ἀκονόπετρα;
Ποιὸς καβαλάρης ἦρθε
μὲ τὸ προσάναμμα καὶ τὸ δαυλό;
Καθένας νίβει τὰ χέρια του
καὶ τὰ δροσίζει.
Καὶ ποιὸς ξεκοίλιασε
τὴ γυναίκα τὸ βρέφος καὶ τὸ σπίτι;
Ἔνοχος δὲν ὑπάρχει, καπνός.
Ποιὸς ἔφυγε
χτυπώντας πέταλα στὶς πλάκες;
Κατάργησαν τὰ μάτια τους· τυφλοί.
Μάρτυρες δὲν ὑπάρχουν πιά, γιὰ τίποτε.

5.

Who heard at high noon
the knife's hiss across the whetstone?
Who came on horseback
with kindling and torch?
Everyone washes his hands
to cool them.
And who disemboweled
the woman, the baby, the house?
There is no culprit: vanished.
Who fled,
clattering hooves over the stones?
They canceled their eyes: blind.
There are no more witnesses, for anything.

Πότε θὰ ξαναμιλήσεις;
Εἶναι παιδιὰ πολλῶν ἀνθρώπων τὰ λόγια μας.
Σπέρνουνται γεννιοῦνται σὰν τὰ βρέφη
ριζώνουν θρέφουνται μὲ τὸ αἶμα.
Ὅπως τὰ πεῦκα
κρατοῦνε τὴ μορφὴ τοῦ ἀγέρα
ἐνῶ ὁ ἀγέρας ἔφυγε, δὲν εἶναι ἐκεῖ
τὸ ἴδιο τὰ λόγια
φυλάγουν τὴ μορφὴ τοῦ ἀνθρώπου
κι' ὁ ἄνθρωπος ἔφυγε, δὲν εἶναι ἐκεῖ.
Ἴσως γυρεύουν νὰ μιλήσουν τ' ἄστρα
ποὺ πάτησαν τὴν τόση γύμνια σου μιὰ νύχτα
ὁ Κύκνος ὁ Τοξότης ὁ Σκορπιὸς
ἴσως ἐκεῖνα.
Ἀλλὰ ποῦ θά εἶσαι τὴ στιγμὴ ποὺ θά 'ρθει
ἐδῶ σ' αὐτὸ τὸ θέατρο τὸ φῶς;

6.

When will you speak again?
They are children of many men, our words.
They are sown and brought forth like infants;
they take root and are nourished with blood.
As pines
keep the shape of the wind
even when the wind has fled and is no longer there,
so words
guard the shape of man
even when man has fled and is no longer there.
Perhaps the stars seek to speak
which trod upon your nakedness one night —
the Swan, the Archer, the Scorpion —
perhaps those.
But where will you be at the moment when,
here in this theater, the light comes on?

Z'

Κι' ὅμως ἐκεῖ, στὴν ἄλλην ὄχθη
κάτω ἀπ' τὸ μαῦρο βλέμμα τῆς σπηλιᾶς
ἥλιοι στὰ μάτια πουλιὰ στοὺς ὤμους
εἴσουν ἐκεῖ· πονοῦσες
τὸν ἄλλο μόχθο τὴν ἀγάπη
τὴν ἄλλη αὐγὴ τὴν παρουσία
τὴν ἄλλη γέννα τὴν ἀνάσταση·
κι' ὅμως ἐκεῖ ξαναγινόσουν
στὴν ὑπέρογκη διαστολὴ τοῦ καιροῦ
στιγμὴ στιγμὴ σὰν τὸ ρετσίνι
τὸ σταλαχτίτη τὸ σταλαγμίτη.

7.

And yet there, on the other shore,
under the dark gaze of the cave —
sun in the eyes, birds on the shoulders —
you were there; you suffered
the other pain, love,
the other dawn, presence,
the other birth, resurrection;
and yet there you were created again
in the vast diastole of time,
drop by drop, like resin,
the stalactite, the stalagmite.

ΘΕΡΙΝΟ ΗΛΙΟΣΤΑΣΙ

SUMMER SOLSTICE

Α΄

Ὁ μεγαλύτερος ἥλιος ἀπὸ τὴ μιὰ μεριὰ
κι᾽ ἀπὸ τὴν ἄλλη τὸ νέο φεγγάρι
ἀπόμακρα στὴ μνήμη σὰν ἐκεῖνα τὰ στήθη.
Ἀνάμεσό τους χάσμα τῆς ἀστερωμένης νύχτας
κατακλυσμὸς τῆς ζωῆς.

Τ᾽ ἄλογα στ᾽ ἀλώνια
καλπάζουν καὶ ἱδρώνουν
πάνω σὲ σκόρπια κορμιά.
Ὅλα πηγαίνουν ἐκεῖ
καὶ τούτη ἡ γυναίκα
ποὺ τὴν εἶδες ὄμορφη, μιὰ στιγμὴ
λυγίζει δὲν ἀντέχει πιὰ γονάτισε.
Ὅλα τ᾽ ἀλέθουν οἱ μυλόπετρες
καὶ γίνονται ἄστρα.

Παραμονὴ τῆς μακρύτερης μέρας.

1.

The greatest sun from one side
and from the other the new moon,
remote in the memory as those breasts.
Between them, the gulf of star-filled night,
inundation of life.

On the threshing-floor the horses
gallop and sweat
over scattered bodies.
Everything goes there;
even this woman,
whom you saw, for a moment, beautiful,
bends, endures no longer, succumbs.
Everything is ground by the millstones
and turned into stars.

Eve of the longest day.

Β΄

Ὅλοι βλέπουν ὁράματα
κανεὶς ὡστόσο δὲν τ' ὁμολογεῖ·
πηγαίνουν καὶ θαροῦν πὼς εἶναι μόνοι.
Τὸ μεγάλο τριαντάφυλλο
εἴτανε πάντα ἐδῶ
στὸ πλευρό σου βαθιὰ μέσα στὸν ὕπνο
δικό σου καὶ ἄγνωστο.
Ἀλλὰ μονάχα τώρα ποὺ τὰ χείλια σου τ' ἄγγιξαν
στ' ἀπώτατα φύλλα
ἔνιωσες τὸ πυκνὸ βάρος τοῦ χορευτῆ
νὰ πέφτει στὸ ποτάμι τοῦ καιροῦ —
τὸ φοβερὸ παφλασμό.

Μὴ σπαταλᾶς τὴν πνοὴ ποὺ σοῦ χάρισε
τούτη ἡ ἀνάσα.

2.

All see visions,
yet no one will confess them;
they go thinking they are alone.
The great rose
was always here
at your side, deep in sleep,
your own and unknown.
But only now that your lips have touched
its outermost petals
have you felt the dense weight of the dancer
as he falls into the river of time —
the terrible ripples.

Do not waste the breath
this breathing has granted you.

Γ´

Κι᾽ ὅμως σ᾽ αὐτὸ τὸν ὕπνο
τ᾽ ὄνειρο ξεπέφτει τόσο εὔκολα
στὸ βραχνά.
῍Οπως τὸ ψάρι ποὺ ἄστραψε κάτω ἀπ᾽ τὸ κύμα
καὶ χώθηκε στὸ βοῦρκο τοῦ βυθοῦ
ἢ χαμαιλέοντας ὅταν ἀλλάζει χρῶμα.
Στὴν πολιτεία ποὺ ἔγινε πορνεῖο
μαστροποὶ καὶ πολιτικιὲς
διαλαλοῦν σάπια θέλγητρα·
ἡ κυματόφερτη κόρη
φορεῖ τὸ πετσὶ τῆς γελάδας
γιὰ νὰ τὴν ἀνεβεῖ τὸ ταυρόπουλο·
ὁ ποιητὴς
χαμίνια τοῦ πετοῦν μαγαρισιὲς
καθὼς βλέπει τ᾽ ἀγάλματα νὰ στάζουν αἷμα.
Πρέπει νὰ βγεῖς ἀπὸ τοῦτο τὸν ὕπνο·
τοῦτο τὸ μαστιγωμένο δέρμα.

3.

And yet in this sleep
the dream degenerates so easily
into nightmare.
Like the fish that flashed under the wave
and plunged to the mud of the depths,
or the chameleon when he changes color.
In the city that has become a brothel
pandars and whores
proclaim rotten charms;
the wave-borne maiden
wears the hide of a cow
so that the young bull will mount her;
the poet —
brats in the street fling shit at him,
while he watches the statues drip blood.
You must come out of this sleep,
out of this scourged skin.

Δ´

Στὸ τρελὸ ἀνεμοσκόρπισμα
δεξιὰ ζερβὰ πάνω καὶ κάτω
στροβιλίζουνται σαρίδια.
Φτενοὶ θανατεροὶ καπνοὶ
λύνουν τὰ μέλη τῶν ἀνθρώπων.
Οἱ ψυχὲς
βιάζουνται ν' ἀποχωριστοῦν τὸ σῶμα
διψοῦν καὶ δὲ βρίσκουν νερὸ πουθενά·
κολνοῦν ἐδῶ κολνοῦν ἐκεῖ στὴν τύχη
πουλιὰ στὶς ξόβεργες·
σπαράζουν ἀνωφέλευτα
ὅσο ποὺ δὲ σηκώνουν ἄλλο τὰ φτερά τους.

Φυραίνει ὁ τόπος ὁλοένα
χωματένιο σταμνί.

4.

On the wind's crazy tossing,
right, left, up, down,
refuse is whirled.
Thin deadly fumes
paralyze men's limbs.
The souls
hasten to leave the body,
thirst and nowhere find water;
they stick here, stick there, at random,
like birds in lime;
they struggle in vain
until they can no longer raise their wings.

The land is ceaselessly desiccated:
an earthen jar.

Ὁ κόσμος τυλιγμένος στὰ ναρκωτικὰ σεντόνια
δὲν ἔχει τίποτε ἄλλο νὰ προσφέρει
παρὰ τοῦτο τὸ τέρμα.
                    Στὴ ζεστὴ νύχτα
ἡ μαραμένη ἱέρεια τῆς Ἑκάτης
μὲ γυμνωμένα στήθη ψηλὰ στὸ δῶμα
παρακαλᾶ μιὰ τεχνητὴ πανσέληνο, καθὼς
δυὸ ἀνήλικες δοῦλες ποὺ χασμουριοῦνται
ἀναδεύουν σὲ μπακιρένια χύτρα
ἀρωματισμένες φαρμακεῖες.
Αὔριο θὰ χορτάσουν ὅσοι ἀγαποῦν τὰ μυρωδικά.

Τὸ πάθος της καὶ τὰ φτιασίδια
εἶναι ὅμοια μὲ τῆς τραγωδοῦ
ὁ γύψος τους μάδησε κιόλας.

5.

The world wrapped in its torpid sheets
has nothing to offer
but this end.
                    In the hot night
the withered priestess of Hecate,
her breasts naked, high on the roof,
entreats an artificial full moon, while
two young slave girls, yawning,
mix in a copper cauldron
aromatic drugs.
Tomorrow, those who delight in perfumes will glut
      themselves.

Her passion and her maquillage
are those of a tragic actress.
Their plaster has worn off already.

Κάτω στὶς δάφνες
κάτω στὶς ἄσπρες πικροδάφνες
κάτω στὸν ἀγκαθερὸ βράχο
κι᾽ ἡ θάλασσα στὰ πόδια μας γυάλινη.
Θυμήσου τὸ χιτῶνα ποὺ ἔβλεπες
ν᾽ ἀνοίγει καὶ νὰ ξεγλιστρᾶ πάνω στὴ γύμνια
κι᾽ ἔπεσε γύρω στοὺς ἀστραγάλους
νεκρὸς —
ἂν ἔπεφτε ἔτσι αὐτὸς ὁ ὕπνος
ἀνάμεσα στὶς δάφνες τῶν νεκρῶν.

6.

Among the laurels,
among the white oleanders,
on the thorny rock,
and the glassy sea at our feet.
Remember the robe you saw
open and slip over nakedness
and fall about the ankles,
dead —
if only this sleep had fallen so
among the laurels of the dead.

Ἡ λεύκα στὸ μικρὸ περιβόλι
ἡ ἀνάσα της μετρᾶ τὶς ὦρες σου
μέρα καὶ νύχτα·
κλεψύδρα ποὺ γεμίζει ὁ οὐρανός.
Στὴ δύναμη τοῦ φεγγαριοῦ τὰ φύλλα της
σέρνουν μαῦρα πατήματα στὸν ἄσπρο τοῖχο.
Στὸ σύνορο εἶναι λιγοστὰ τὰ πεῦκα
ἔπειτα μάρμαρα καὶ φωταψίες
κι᾽ ἄνθρωποι καθὼς εἶναι πλασμένοι οἱ ἄνθρωποι.
Ὁ κότσυφας ὅμως τιτιβίζει
σὰν ἔρχεται νὰ πιεῖ
κι᾽ ἀκοῦς καμιὰ φορὰ φωνὴ τῆς δεκοχτούρας.

Στὸ μικρὸ περιβόλι δέκα δρασκελιὲς
μπορεῖς νὰ ἰδεῖς τὸ φῶς τοῦ ἥλιου
νὰ πέφτει σὲ δυὸ κόκκινα γαρούφαλλα
σὲ μιὰν ἐλιὰ καὶ λίγο ἀγιόκλημα.

Δέξου ποιὸς εἶσαι.
                    Τὸ ποίημα
μὴν τὸ καταποντίζεις στὰ βαθιὰ πλατάνια
θρέψε το μὲ τὸ χῶμα καὶ τὸ βράχο ποὺ ἔχεις.
Τὰ περισσότερα —
σκάψε στὸν ἴδιο τόπο νὰ τὰ βρεῖς.

7.

The poplar tree in the little garden,
its breathing marks your hours
night and day:
a sky-filled clepsydra.
Under the moon's brightness its leaves
drag black footsteps across the white wall.
On the border, a few pines,
then fragments of marble and the lights of the city
and people — the way people usually are.
Yet the blackbird twitters
when it comes to drink,
and at times you hear the voice of the ringdove.

Ten steps in the little garden:
you can see the sunlight
fall on two red carnations,
on an olive tree and a bit of honeysuckle.

Accept who you are.
                    The poem,
do not cast it down under the thick plane trees;
nourish it with the earth and rock you have.
For better things —
dig the same ground to find them.

H´

T᾽ ἄσπρο χαρτὶ σκληρὸς καθρέφτης
ἐπιστρέφει μόνο ἐκεῖνο ποὺ εἴσουν.

T᾽ ἄσπρο χαρτὶ μιλᾶ μὲ τὴ φωνή σου,
τὴ δική σου φωνὴ
ὄχι ἐκείνη ποὺ σ᾽ ἀρέσει·
μουσική σου εἶναι ἡ ζωὴ
αὐτὴ ποὺ σπατάλησες.
Μπορεῖ νὰ τὴν ξανακερδίσεις ἂν τὸ θέλεις
ἂν καρφωθεῖς σὲ τοῦτο τ᾽ ἀδιάφορο πρᾶγμα
ποὺ σὲ ρίχνει πίσω
ἐκεῖ ποὺ ξεκίνησες.

Ταξίδεψες, εἶδες πολλὰ φεγγάρια πολλοὺς ἥλιους
ἄγγιξες νεκροὺς καὶ ζωντανοὺς
ἔνιωσες τὸν πόνο τοῦ παλικαριοῦ
καὶ τὸ βογγητὸ τῆς γυναίκας
τὴν πίκρα τοῦ ἄγουρου παιδιοῦ —
ὅ,τι ἔνιωσες σωριάζεται ἀνυπόστατο
ἂν δὲν ἐμπιστευτεῖς τοῦτο τὸ κενό.
Ἴσως νὰ βρεῖς ἐκεῖ ὅ,τι νόμισες χαμένο·
τὴ βλάστηση τῆς νιότης, τὸ δίκαιο καταποντισμὸ
        τῆς ἡλικίας.

Ζωή σου εἶναι ὅ,τι ἔδωσες
τοῦτο τὸ κενὸ εἶναι ὅ,τι ἔδωσες
τὸ ἄσπρο χαρτί.

8.

The blank page, difficult mirror,
gives back only what you were.

The blank page speaks with your voice,
your own voice,
not the one you like;
your music is this life
you wasted.
You could regain it if you wish,
if you fasten to this indifferent thing
which casts you back
there where you set out.

You have journeyed, have seen many moons, many suns,
have touched the dead and the living,
have known the sorrow of the young man
and the groans of the woman,
the bitterness of the boy —
all you have experienced falls in an insubstantial heap
if you do not trust this void.
Perhaps you will find there what you thought lost:
the flowering of youth, the rightful sinking of age.

Your life is what you gave:
this void is what you gave:
the blank page.

Θ´

Μιλοῦσες γιὰ πράγματα ποὺ δὲν τά 'βλεπαν
κι' αὐτοὶ γελούσαν.

῎Ομως νὰ λάμνεις στὸ σκοτεινὸ ποταμὸ
πάνω νερά·
νὰ πηγαίνεις στὸν ἀγνοημένο δρόμο
στὰ τυφλά, πεισματάρης
καὶ νὰ γυρεύεις λόγια ριζωμένα
σὰν τὸ πολύροζο λιόδεντρο —
ἄφησε κι' ἂς γελοῦν.
Καὶ νὰ ποθεῖς νὰ κατοικήσει κι' ὁ ἄλλος κόσμος
στὴ σημερινὴ πνιγερὴ μοναξιὰ
στ' ἀφανισμένο τοῦτο παρὸν —
ἄφησέ τους.

῾Ο θαλασσινὸς ἄνεμος κι' ἡ δροσιὰ τῆς αὐγῆς
ὑπάρχουν χωρὶς νὰ τὸ ζητήσει κανένας.

9.

You spoke of things they did not see,
and they laughed.

Yet to row on the dark river,
against the current;
to go along the unknown road
blindly, obstinately,
and to seek words rooted
like the many-knotted olive tree —
let them laugh.
And to long that those of the other world should inhabit
today's stifling loneliness,
this ruined time —
forget them.

The sea wind and the coolness of dawn
exist without being sought.

Ι΄

Τὴν ὥρα ποὺ τὰ ὀνείρατα ἀληθεύουν
στὸ γλυκοχάραμα τῆς μέρας
εἶδα τὰ χείλια ποὺ ἄνοιγαν
φύλλο τὸ φύλλο.

Ἔλαμπε ἕνα λιγνὸ δρεπάνι στὸν οὐρανό.
Φοβήθηκα μὴν τὰ θερίσει.

10.

At the hour when dreams come true,
at the first sweet glimmer of dawn,
I saw lips that opened
leaf by leaf.

A slim sickle shone in the sky.
I feared it would mow them down.

ΙΑ΄

Ἡ θάλασσα ποὺ ὀνομάζουν γαλήνη
πλεούμενα κι᾿ ἄσπρα πανιὰ
μπάτης ἀπὸ τὰ πεῦκα καὶ τ᾿ Ὄρος τῆς Αἴγινας
λαχανιασμένη ἀνάσα·
τὸ δέρμα σου γλιστροῦσε στὸ δέρμα της
εὔκολο καὶ ζεστὸ
σκέψη σχεδὸν ἀκάμωτη κι᾿ ἀμέσως ξεχασμένη.

Μὰ στὰ ρηχὰ
ἕνα καμακωμένο χταπόδι τίναξε μελάνι
καὶ στὸ βυθὸ —
ἂν συλλογιζόσουν ὣς ποὺ τελειώνουν τὰ ὄμορφα νησιά.

Σὲ κοίταζα μ᾿ ὅλο τὸ φῶς καὶ τὸ σκοτάδι ποὺ ἔχω.

11.

The sea that they call calm,
ships and white sails,
sea breeze from the pines and the Mount of Aéghina,
panting breath;
your skin slippery on hers,
easy and warm;
thought almost half-formed and at once forgotten.

But in the shallows
a speared octopus pulsed out its ink,
and in the depths —
if you could think where the beautiful islands end.

I watched you with all the light and darkness I have.

IB´

Τὸ αἷμα τώρα τινάζεται
καθὼς φουσκώνει ἡ κάψα
στὶς φλέβες τ᾿ οὐρανοῦ τ᾿ ἀφορμισμένου.
Γυρεύει νὰ περάσει ἀπὸ τὸ θάνατο
γιὰ νά ᾿βρει τὴ χαρά.

Τὸ φῶς εἶναι σφυγμὸς
ὁλοένα πιὸ ἀργὸς καὶ πιὸ ἀργὸς
θαρεῖς πὼς πάει νὰ σταματήσει.

12.

The blood shudders now
as the heat swells
in the veins of the inflamed sky.
It seeks to pass beyond death
to find joy.

The light is a pulse
ever slower and slower.
It seems it is going to stop altogether.

ΙΓ´

Λίγο ἀκόμη καὶ θὰ σταματήσει ὁ ἥλιος.
Τὰ ξωτικὰ τῆς αὐγῆς
φύσηξαν στὰ στεγνὰ κοχύλια·
τὸ πουλὶ κελάιδησε τρεῖς φορὲς τρεῖς φορὲς μόνο·
ἡ σαύρα πάνω στὴν ἄσπρη πέτρα
μένει ἀκίνητη
κοιτάζοντας τὸ φρυγμένο χόρτο
ἐκεῖ ποὺ γλίστρησε ἡ δεντρογαλιά.
Μαύρη φτερούγα σέρνει ἔνα βαθὺ χαράκι
ψηλὰ στὸ θόλο τοῦ γαλάζιου —
δές τον, θ' ἀνοίξει.

Ἀναστάσιμη ὠδίνη.

13.

A little more, and the sun will cease.
The ghosts of dawn
blew through the dry shells;
the bird sang out thrice and thrice only;
the lizard on the white stone
sits motionless,
watching the scorched grass
there where an adder glides.
A black wing drags a deep cut
high across the dome of blue sky —
watch: it will open.

Birth pang of resurrection.

ΙΔ΄

Τώρα,
μὲ τὸ λυωμένο μολύβι τοῦ κλήδονα
τὸ λαμπύρισμα τοῦ καλοκαιρινοῦ πελάγου,
ἡ γύμνια ὁλόκληρης τῆς ζωῆς·
καὶ τὸ πέρασμα καὶ τὸ σταμάτημα καὶ
        τὸ πλάγιασμα καὶ τὸ τίναγμα
τὰ χείλια τὸ χαϊδεμένο δέρας,
ὅλα γυρεύουν νὰ καοῦν.

Ὅπως τὸ πεῦκο καταμεσήμερα
κυριεμένο ἀπ᾽ τὸ ρετσίνι
βιάζεται νὰ γεννήσει φλόγα
καὶ δὲ βαστᾶ πιὰ τὴν παιδωμὴ —

φώναξε τὰ παιδιὰ νὰ μαζέψουν τὴ στάχτη
καὶ νὰ τὴ σπείρουν.
Ὅ,τι πέρασε πέρασε σωστά.

Κι᾽ ἐκεῖνα ἀκόμη ποὺ δὲν πέρασαν
πρέπει νὰ καοῦν
τοῦτο τὸ μεσημέρι ποὺ καρφώθηκε ὁ ἥλιος
στὴν καρδιὰ τοῦ ἑκατόφυλλου ρόδου.

14.

Now,
with the molten lead of divination,
with the shimmering of the summer sea,
the nakedness of the whole of life;
and the passing and the stopping,
    the bending and the darting,
the lips, the caressed skin —
everything wants to burn.

As the pine tree at high noon,
overcome with resin,
hurries to give birth to flames
and endures the pangs no longer —

call the children to gather the ashes
and sow them.
What is gone is rightly gone.

And whatever is not yet gone
must be burned
in this noon when the sun is nailed
to the heart of the centifoliate rose.

NOTES   ACKNOWLEDGMENTS

NOTES

page 7, line 2: In Greek mythology, the Graiae were the daughters of Phorcys and Ceto, named Pemphredo, Enyo, and Deino, and the Gorgons were their sisters. Goddesses of the white sea foam, they were, according to Hesiod (*Theogony*, 271), white-haired from birth.

page 17, line 11: See Heraclitus, fr. 64 (Diels), τὰ δὲ πάντα οἰακίζει Κεραυνός, "Lightning steers all things."

page 21, line 5: See G. Chortatzes, *Erophile*, III.i.8. The *Erophile* is the longest, bloodiest, and most famous of the Cretan Renaissance tragedies. Seferis has always considered this play and Cornaro's epic, *Erotocritos*, both of which date from the early seventeenth century, as two of the greatest monuments of modern Greek poetry. He quotes this same passage in his essay, "Monologue on Poetry," where he says: "There is no royal road . . . that leads straight to poetry . . . After one has known the great works, has familiarized himself with them, has made them his blood and the marrow of his bones, after he has cultivated and strengthened his poetic sensitivity, he should know that there will come a moment in which he will be alone, without the help of gods or men, naked, whether he is a poet or a lover of poetry: 'as if I had to pass through / an angry sea or some wild forest.' And it pleases me that this sense of a dark forest, a 'selva oscura,' is found at the very beginning of one of the centuries' poetic pinnacles, since it is the threshold of

67

every poetic experience." Δοκιμές, 2nd ed. (Athens, 1962), pp. 130–131.

page 25, line 10: A lunar and chthonian goddess of ancient and obscure origin, sometimes confused with Artemis, Hecate was a powerful and often highly beneficent deity. But she was also associated with dark magic and the world of ghosts, and as a result she was worshiped at crossroads, which have been haunted places to many primitive imaginations. Since a crossroad is normally a juncture of a side path and a main road, she was often pictured by classical antiquity as having three faces. See Hesiod, *Theogony*, 411ff.

page 27, line 16: According to Homer, the Old Man of the Seas is Proteus of Egypt (*Odyssey*, IV.384ff). The eastern end of the Mediterranean was sometimes known as the Sea of Proteus.

page 37, line 15: See note for page 63, line 2.

page 57, line 3: Aéghina — the spelling attempts to indicate how it is pronounced in Modern Greek; it is normally spelled Aegina — is an island in the Saronic Gulf visible from parts of Athens.

page 63, line 2: The summer solstice, which provides this third poem with its title, occurs at the time of the Feast of St. John (June 24), which is one of the most important festivals in Greece. The feast day is variously known as that of St. John of the Solstice, St. John Lambrophoros, or St. John the Diviner, because of the divinatory customs (*cledonisma*) practiced on this occasion. One such custom is the dropping of molten lead into a container of "speechless" water — that is, water which a child has carried secretly from a well without speaking to or answering anyone met on the way. The future is foretold from the shape the lead assumes when it hardens in water.

G. A. Megas, *Greek Calendar Customs* (Athens, 1963), pp. 134–135, describes the custom of lighting bonfires on the eve of this feast: "The village boys gather timber, twigs, dry leaves, and bramble for the bonfire . . . The fire is lighted at sunset. The whole neighbourhood then begin dancing round it, holding hands. When the flames reach the trunk, it is thrown down and the dancers begin leaping over flames . . . When the fire has gone out completely, the village women scoop up a handful of ashes, to take home for protective and divinatory purposes. Various wishes and prayers are said during the leaping of the fire, such as: 'I leave the bad year behind in order to enter a better year,' or 'I leap over the fire so that sickness will not touch me,' or 'Dear St. John, may I be cured,' which proves that the ancient significance of leaping over a fire — purification from all evil by the power of fire — still unconsciously survives in the popular imagination." In addition to Megas, for another account of *cledonisma*, see J. T. Bent, *The Cyclades, or Life among the Insular Greeks*, ed. A. N. Oikonomides (Chicago, 1966), pp. 160–163, which is cited by Frazer in his great edition of Pausanias; also, J. C. Lawson, *Modern Greek Folklore and Ancient Greek Religion*, introd. A. N. Oikonomides (New Hyde Park, N.Y., 1964). Of particular interest in this connection is Seferis' earlier poem, "Fires of St. John," in *Collected Poems, 1924–1955*, trans., ed., and introd. by Edmund Keeley and Philip Sherrard (Princeton, 1967), pp. 126–129.

ACKNOWLEDGMENTS

With uncommon patience and generosity, George Seferis has commented on successive versions of this translation. Only someone who was himself a very great translator could have supplied such sensitive, helpful answers as he has to my innumerable questions, and I am as grateful to him for them as I am for the delightful series of letters they occasioned. I must also express my gratitude to Athan Anagnostopoulos and Cedric Whitman who, with their careful criticisms of a first draft, saved me from a number of errors.

Sadly, the expression of my greatest thanks must go unread by the recipient. Dudley Fitts, beloved friend and teacher for many years, took a special interest in this translation and offered, with customary wit, invaluable advice and encouragement; the final version received his approval only a few days before his unexpected and untimely death. He had a greater understanding of the art of translation and a surer sense of the ways of poetry than anyone I have ever known, and his loss is both a personal one and a loss for poetry itself.

W.K.

Seal Harbor
August, 1968